God's Ribbons

by Cynthia Watts

May 'God's Ribbons' bring you
peace, comfort and hope as
you continue your life's
journey —

Blessings —

Cynthia Friedman
Watts

Library of Congress Control Number: 2001119939

ISBN: 1-57579-237-0

Cover art by Doug Moss

First printing, 2001
Second printing, 2004

For books or speaking engagements,
please contact:
God's Ribbons
cindyannf@hotmail.com
605-366-0963

Printed in the United States of America

PINE HILL PRESS
4000 West 57th Street
Sioux Falls, S.D. 57106

God's Ribbons

God's Ribbons wove their way through my heart and soul, and eventually, through my writing in the spring of the year 2000. It seems God patiently waited for me to be calm, quiet and still before he wrapped his ribbons of love and healing around my wounded soul and being. You see, I was living in the aftermath of the death of my mother five months earlier. I had not allowed myself to truly grieve her death. I thrust myself back into my work and continued on my hectic way. I believe now that I was running away from the pain that my grieving would bring. So, I simply did not allow it. It seems that God let me go on like that until six months later. Then he simply laid me temporarily on my back so his soft ribbons could wrap around my heartbreak and my wounded soul. It was then that the healing began.

I felt the first soft strand intertwine through my thoughts while recovering from a minor back problem, while lying down in our car in a parking lot awaiting my husband's return.

Soft and gentle words appeared to my mind's eye.

I could not hear them, only see them. Short gatherings of words at first. It seems they were impatiently waiting for me to get them down on paper. While laying down in the car. I could see clouds, beautiful...white, fluffy clouds floating by. As I was watching them the words 'Heaven's Door' appeared in my mind. I could actually see the words. Quickly scribbling the words down, I could not believe how quickly they came, tumbling one over another. When the words stopped coming I had written a sweet little poem entitled, "Heaven's Door". Thinking how nice that was, and wondering where in the world did it come from, I could not have been prepared for what was yet to come.

When my husband returned I told him what had happened and read the poem to him. He looked at me with surprise and asked, "Do you do that?" I told him, "No, I do not write poetry. And I have no idea where it came from!"

III

As we began our drive home, through the country, still laying down, watching more clouds, darker and different than the first, more words came to me. I could see the words "The Week the Angels Came" and scavenged for paper once more. Writing as quickly as I could, words began to pour out without stopping. As we arrived home, the words were still coming. I almost ran into the house to turn on my laptop computer and typed as quickly as I could to get the words down. What flowed through my fingers, was the most beautiful recapture of my mother's final week on earth, as she visited with angels her entire last week as she succumbed to cancer.

This happened on a Saturday evening. The following Monday, while having lunch with a dear friend, I told him of the experience and showed him the poem, The Week the Angels Came. He was quite astounded. He asked me what I was going to do with it. I told him I didn't know what to do with it or what to make of the situation. I did tell him that I planned to show it to a friend, who is a pastor, perhaps the next day. I was headed for home after working a half-day, still recuperating from my back problem. I needed to go home to rest. As I climbed into my van to head for home, I could not go there. I was compelled to drive directly to the church to show this to Pastor Don Lehmann at Our Savior's Lutheran Church. Pastor Lehmann had handled both of my parent's funerals. He also visited my mother at home during that incredible week. I visited with the church receptionist and learned that he was preparing for a funeral service. I told her not to disturb him and asked if I could leave him a message. As I turned to leave, something made me turn back around and ask her if she would please see that he received my note and the poem "The Week the Angels Came" before the funeral service. She looked at me rather quizzically but said that she would.

As I was about to drive out of the parking lot I heard pounding on the side of my van. It was Pastor Lehmann. He had chased me down! I told him I knew he was preparing for a funeral service and did not want to disturb him. I also asked him if he had seen what I had left for him. He said that he had not had a chance to look at it but wanted to catch me before I left. I quickly told him about how the poem came to me and asked that he look at it before the funeral service if possible. He said he would do so. An hour and a half later my phone rang. It was Pastor Lehmann. His words to me were, " How did you know?" I told him that I didn't know anything but asked him what happened. He said he read "The Week the Angels Came" at the funeral service and told the guests how he came upon the poem, chasing me down in the parking lot. The funeral was for a mother of five daughters and according to him the poem was a beautiful gift for them and how it had touched their hearts. It seems they had had a similar experience during their mother's dying experience. I felt chills of humbling joy and thanked God for giving me the gift of this poem that could help to ease someone else's grief. I received a beautiful letter from one of the daughters and my heart was humbly and joyfully touched once again.

That was the beginning.

The beginning of the most beautiful journey I have ever taken in my life. It began slowly and gathered speed to the point that at one moment I was seeing the words to several different poems at once. It was incredible!

These messages, I truly believe, are a gift that was sent through my heart and soul, to help me cope with my grief and pain. I also believe that while they were sent through me to sooth my sorrow and heal my aching heart, they are also meant to be shared with others whose hearts and souls may also be on a painful journey. And perhaps to give hope and encouragement to people in need of comfort.

All in all, the first sixty poems of "God's Ribbons" came to me within a three-week period of time. I was immobile, wrapped in 'God's Ribbons'. I was quiet and still. God had my attention. And I listened.

I think others will also hear His gentle whispers, the soft words he placed upon my heart, as they begin to unwrap 'God's Ribbons'.

Enjoy.

Dedication

"God's Ribbons" is dedicated to my mother, Lillian Evadna Kjenstad Watts, through whose life, I was given this beautiful gift wrapped with "God's Ribbons".

The following two poems, "The Week the Angels Came" and "God's Hand on Me" will acquaint you with my journey through God's beautiful strands of ribbons.

The Week the Angels Came

The week the angels came we were simply unaware.....that they would come, yes, really come ... not how & when & where

They came so softly and so sweet, we simply weren't prepared For times so sweet, times so complete. The days that we would share.

The angels sang such sweet, sweet songs... they surely did belong Belong to us, our kin, our own. We knew them one by one.

We stood in awe, on holy ground, we could not say a word. But, Mother heard, oh, how she heard. Of this we were so sure.

Their song went on for days and days, music our ears could not hear. But, they were there, for sure they were! They were so very near.

Through Mom's bright eyes we saw their face, their voice, through hers, I swear. Their very words were shared with us that day, right then and there.

We stood in awe and realized we did not need to pray. We lived prayer now, I know not how...but it was real that day. We witnessed joy and peace and calm I cannot tell you how.

Their words through hers were soft and sweet and laughter did abound. A sense of humor shared by all was there on holy ground.

Questions asked were answered not in words our ears could hear. Cloaked in grace behind the veil they'll wait for us some year.

We tried to see through Mother's eyes, the wonders for ourselves. The angels laughed, I think, that day to see us peek and peer. We know they smiled at us that day, my mother told us so. We could not grasp they were so close, so great, so near right here.

The "Boys" came first, six of them, in all. Then came Dad, and more and more and everyone was tall! Mom spoke to them without a break. She would not rest you see, they came to take her home with them. She tried to help us see.

We tried too hard to see them clear. Our fear was that they'd leave before we got to know them. How silly soon we'd feel. Mom's visions, to us, would simply not be revealed.

They're always here, we came to know, as sure as apple pie. They live on earth among us all, not somewhere in the sky.

We walked among them that sweet week with knowledge they were here. The difference was, we took the time..... were still enough to hear.

Their kindnesses were patient ones, Mom would not go at first. She shook her head, said "No" a lot. They waited now and first. Her sisters came, and Roger too, we sat in awe of this. What joy we had, she had it too, so near eternal bliss.

She talked to "Ma" and then to "Pa" and "Grandma" came at last. It seems her words were heard the best because Mom would not long last. Soon after my mother's grandma's touch my mother left this earth.

We hugged and cried as Mother died. How could we go on now? We can, you see, cause mother's love stays with us here and now!

Written by Cynthia Watts on May 20, 2000 about her mother's final week on earth.

Lillian Kjenstad Watts died at her home October 10,1999 after a six month struggle with ovarian cancer.

God's Hand on Me

As my mother died
I cried and I cried
Once gone, I went back to my life
Acting as if nothing was wrong

Life's pace escalated
My time was all sated
I carried on stoically and strong

Until the nighttime when sleep would not find me
And peace would not calm me at all
I rested not for many a month
And little did soothing sleep call

I lived with illusion of facing this trial
Of grief and of sorrow just waiting
I acted like all was well with my spirit
But I was just evading

God tried to catch my eye
He whispered in my ear
He tapped on my shoulder too

I just turned away
I did not want to hear
Whatever he had to say

He sighed, 'allright now',
And then, laid me flat on my back
So, I would hear him calling
His message I could no longer slack

Through my heart
He asked me to share the messages
That he sent from his holy heart

At first I did not listen
My mind was set on me
But his hand was on my heart
Very soon that was all I could see

Soft words he gently placed
On my pain
And they came right through

X

His heart to my soul
To be shared with everyone anew

It was really quite astounding
I felt God's loving me grounding

The words, they came, quickly tumbling out
So fast I could hardly keep
Placing them upon paper
They even came through my sleep

My heart was filled with love and with peace
And complete adoration for God
He is using my very life
To tell of his salvation
And the sad road he trod

I've always known that we
All have a mission
But when it's made clear from above
He guides us with his kindness
And wonderful strength-giving love

It's a bit unnerving
And fills me with awe
That he really puts his hand right on us

He loves us so deeply
And wants us to know
It's in us that he's put his trust

With our hearts and minds
And our hands and feet
We are to walk his miles
Sharing with others his love
And his wonderful smiles

Share with all our neighbors, friends
And foes, and those we haven't yet met
Share his love that wraps around us all
With whole or broken hearts

Contents

INSPIRATION

God's Ribbons 2
Loving 4
Our Soul 5
Heart 7
My Father's Music 8
Glimpses of Heaven 9
God's Face 11
Serenity 13
Babies 15
Little Boys 16
The Day We Were Born 18
His Arms 19
Heaven's Door 20
Our Very Own Angels .21
Heroes 22
My Father 23
God's Kids 24
Friends 25
Grandchildren 26
Our Children 27
Our Best Friend 28
Prayer 29
The Gentleness of God 30
One that We Love 31
Our Gift 32

GLIMPSES OF CHRIST

His Father on Earth 36
My Son 38
Our Sin 39
His Feet 40
His Robe 41
The Battle 42
His Breath 43
His Hands 44
His Back 45
His Heart 46
His Blood 47
The Temptation 48

ENCOURAGEMENT AND CONSOLATION

His Ear 50
God's Love 52
His Love 53
Anger 54
Thirst 56
Deep Hunger 57
Trouble 58
Our Tears 60
The Storm 61
The Ocean 62
His Eyes 63
His Kingdom 64
Illness 65
Crossing Rivers 67
Peace 68
Spirit 69
Spirits 70
Food for Our Soul 71
Our Fear 72
God's Link 73
Roads 74
Sorrow 75
Flowers 76
Bridges 78
Places in Time 80
Bridging the Gap 81
Sidewalks 83
Going Home 85
Signs 86
Restless 88
Death 90
Anguish 92
Empty Heart 94

LIFE TODAY

Rocks 96
Waters 98
Young People 99
Winds 101
Windows 102
Our Earth 103
Family 104
Life's Wind 105

My Demons 107
The Lost and the Lonely 108
Fatigue 109
Life 110
Lone Soul 111
In Between 112
Poetry is Dancing 113

CLOSE TO HEART

My Little Girls 116
Grief 117
Heart's Pain 119
Mothers and Daughters 121
Home in my Heart 122

SEASONS

Winter's Whisper 124
The Season 125
The Lonely Couple 126

INSPIRATION

God's Ribbons

God's Ribbons tie up loose corners of our life
They weave in and out of our days

They wind through our hearts and souls
They're what help us remember to pray

Some ribbons are wide, some are narrow
Some satin soft, some of rough rope

They tie our lives together with others we know
And some of them help us to cope

They come in soft colors some in dark hues
Some create beautiful bows

The bows come when life is truly sublime
Knots come when our hands 'up we throw'

Some of the ribbons may fly all askance
God helps us catch all of the ends

When winds come along that are blowing quite strong
Life's ribbon chasing can begin

The strands can be beautiful up in the air
Blowing which way the wind blows

The sun's glint on the fabric may catch your eye
But don't be deceived by the fluttering by

Some kinds of ribbons come not from God's sky
Some cords look like his ribbons up there

They're not always so
They can come
From a very dark place below

Not always aware from whence they come
We pray God will protect us with his sign

By wrapping his ribbons on us all around
His love surely includes
His grace of bright satin ties

That will light up our lives
And awaken our souls from within

God's ribbons wrap 'round the most beautiful gifts
That our eyes will ever behold

These gifts hold our precious heavenly lives
That are just about to unfold

As we walk through his door
And we open them at our life's end

Loving

Do you love with abandon
As if tomorrow may never come
It could be gone in a wink
In the twitch of your little thumb

Open your arms and your heart and your soul
Let loving rush in
And your life will be whole

Little kids' loving knows no bounds
They spread young loving all around
Unless there's a sound
Reason they've found to not

They know loving's powerful
Hold on God's heart
Hold on to his hand
Let loving simply start

To flow in and flow out
All of your days
Loving touches all souls
Soothes all troubles and frays

Loving is all that stays
Forever and on
It never wears out
And lives every one of your days

On this earth and beyond
It carries you through
Ordeals you never believed you'd get through

Loving holds tight
Won't let you go
It will get you through nights
Of storms and yes, stews

So love all you can
Face life with love's face
Soar with God's angels right through heaven's gates

Our Soul

Our soul walks alongside us
As we tarry along
Life's footpath that lies before
As we saunter through our life's song

Our songs are all different
They're all symphonies
To God's heart and his eyes
As he blesses us on our knees

His baton leads us all
If we just play our part
Making life's music
Straight from our heart

It's a tough tune to carry
We all know the drill
Why then, make our lives
Go straight uphill

The incline is steep
Our soul is to keep
Us from taking a nosedive
Right into the deep

Soul searching comes calling
So answer your door
God's love and his Kingdom
Are abundantly in store

For lost souls and broken ones
And strong ones alike
Life's journey can be gloriously more than a hike

Pick up your knapsack, your baggage and trunk
God's right there beside you to carry the bulk
Of worries and sorrows
Disappointments and more

All you have to do is simply answer your door
His arms are wide open

Strong enough for your load
So invite him in to your humble abode

He'll listen for hours
And hold you for more
Your heart and your burden go right to his core
Of love and forgiveness
Warm comfort await too

He'll rejoice when he sees that it's just him and you
Climbing mountains and fording streams
Happiness awaits you both
More than you could possibly dream

Heart

Have heart for those who fall
Not necessarily to their knees

For those who cry with sadness
Whose tomorrow looks quite bleak
And for those who have pain
And unbearable sorrow

On your knees ask God please
Help give them ease
For all of today and tomorrow

His love comforts all
They haven't heard his call
If so they may have just turned away

Not believing it's true
They may see him through you
God needs us to help them this very day

He has been there for us
It's now our turn to trust
That the promise God made is for always

We need to help any way that we can
Help them get through their tomorrows

My Father's Music

My Father's music moves my heart
In incredibly mystical ways
Notes heard only by my soul's ears
Sooth my troubled heart this day

Heartstring's melodies
That only angels can hear
Beckon my very being

The wind's sighing breeze
Through the softly swaying trees
Come closest to the sound

Of Angel's wings brushing God's hem
As it sweeps o'er holy ground

Heavenly hearts soar
At the soft hush
And at the rush
That is felt throughout all of our senses

God's children are finally laying down
Their impenetrable defenses

They are opening God's gate
To release sad hearts deep inside
No more will they cry for solace

They're in God's hands
Now they can fly

Away with the mystical song
That will comfort us all on this earth
When they have left and are gone

Glimpses of Heaven

Gossamer wings, softly gauze things
Gently fly by in our minds
White clouds abound
Nearly everywhere around

Soft mist is fine and quite sublime
Caressing us all as we fall
Right into the lap of God's love

In heaven above
We see all is love

It's almost impossible to believe
That no sorrow lives here
Tears are nowhere
Happiness bursts all your seams

It's beyond all comprehension
The stuff that you've dreamed of
Has landed right here in your lap

Your family is here
You know people from where
You have only heard about
And some that you've heard about not

Generations are sitting right here
Waiting
Simply for you to arrive

It's only in heaven
That you'll realize
Now you are really alive

Joy is abundant
Ecstasy unfolds
It is beyond our wildest dreams

We could not have planned anything like this
Not with our best plans and schemes

Earth's life is meant to be savored
Soak up life's joys while you can
Get ready for exquisite life up in heaven
You'll be amazed at God's wonderful plan

Until you have climbed the great stairway
That leads to the great house of God
Your room awaits your arrival
Your footsteps will easily plod

The glorious path that awaits you
Your life will be a soft thought

God's love brings you here
You'll surely revere
That his son
With his precious life bought

Your life and your soul and your being
You needn't pay for one single thing
He only asks that you love him
And love all others on earth

In only a blink of an eye
You'll come home
From your everyday life on earth

God's Face

God's face smiles on us
In many a way
We may see it in clouds on a summery day

It shines on us all
Each minute we live
If we'd just look around
We'd see it in kids

Kids are God's face smiling
At his best
No wrinkles of time
Grace their tenderest

Minutes of time
That race by in a flash
Catch his face quickly
Kids too soon dash

Hunger reveals God's face through its pain
Sorrow reflects God's face
Filled with rain

When storm clouds float
Through your life
Take a breath and a pause

You'll see his face there
He is there just because

You can rest assured
His face will greet you
Through many a door
He's seen your path coming

And up he will shore
You for all the trials
Awaiting your soul

His face wards off evil
He won't let it through
If your faith rests with him
It is time tested true

The lost and the lonely
Share his demeanor
It's looking through God's mirror
That will make our souls cleaner
Than ever before

He washes their feet
And to us he implores
To do the very same
Walk where he's been

Show his face
To the downtrodden
People within
Your heart's reach
Lift them up

Together we rise
To drink from his cup
Of life giving wine
That will pass through our lips
And down through our souls

Waiting to walk with God's heart on our sleeve
His love to impart
Through our bright smiling face
That mimics the man

Whose face smiles on all
Within his arm's span
His arms reach quite wide
They hold one and all

While joy's tears run down
His face
And on our lives fall

Serenity

Serenity comes when friends gather close
So close to your very being

Sharing life's lope
Just being together

Helps you get through
No matter time's inclement meaning

Pieces of time
Softly land on your soul

When you aren't even looking
They make your life whole

We feel love's soft roll
Over hearts and minds
And yes right over our feelings

We do need the respite
In spite of resolve
To handle how life's got us reeling

Brief moments in time
Reshape things in our mind
We thought could never reshape

God gives us good friends
To help make our ends
Come together
In some sort of reason

God's love has its way
Every single day
If we open our hearts right to it

Hug your friends in your heart
And let time not depart
Your soul from theirs intuit

Let not a day go by in life's fray
Without touching a life
Close around you

Their love will lap over and under and through
Your life's time
God will bless them and you

With bounties so rich and abundant
Unlike anything here on this earth

Our friends are gifts
God gave one and all
He knew we'd need them from birth

They are his way of placing himself
Inside your soul and your being
In a way we accept without question

He lives through them and us
So, what's the fuss
Love your friends without hesitation

Babies

Babies see angels all day long
Just watch them giggle and smile
At nothing at all it appears

They watch them walk slowly all over the place
From their strollers and highchairs

Alone in their cribs
Ever wonder why they gurgle and coo while alone

They're there by themselves, or are they
Think twice and be thankful angels live in your home

Angels love babies more than life itself
They love more than mere mortal man

It's hard to believe they love them more than you
Is it possible that they really can

Angels love us the same wonderful way
We saw them at our life's start

They were talking to us
Sharing wonderful things
Things we have somehow forgot

When did that happen
When we lost it all
Our wonder, our awe of each day

When did we turn the corner
And with the angels no longer play

What a sad day that was, for us and the angels alike

But, rest assured they wait for one and for all
At the end of our road and our life

They helped us begin, they will help us end
Our life on this earth as we know it

They'll fly us on home to our heavenly life
We'll be there before you know it

Little Boys

Little boys come to you all in a tumble
Their smiles just melt your heart

Hair all askew
They're noisy, they rumble
All they want is to be close to you

Hug them and squeeze them
All that you can
Because before you know it
They'll grow into a man

Grown men with babes
Of their very own
It's hard to believe
It seems only yesterday
They cried on your sleeve

Crawled up in your lap
Wanting a kiss
This is as close as we get
To heavenly bliss

Feet covered with mud
They track up your floor
Then run right outside
And bring in even more

The day will come
When you'll yearn for those tracks
What wouldn't we give
To take time back

They were just babies
Dressed all in blue
For everything they needed
They looked right to you

You fed them and clothed them
And nursed them while ill
You climbed every mountain
And pushed them uphill

Our God does this for us
As we did for them
We live in his heart
As our boys do in ours

Time will come
For these little boy men to leave
Now it will be us
Crying upon their sleeve

Fret not they'll return
And bring back the love
You instilled in their hearts
And for which you yearn

You'll never be severed
No matter the chart
Their travels will follow
In tune with their heart

Your prints are embedded
On their hearts and their souls

No matter their future
In warm winds or cold
Your lives are entwined
And God's plan will unfold

Miles may lie
Between thee and he
But heartstrings reach infinitely

So cry not, close your eyes
Rest your heart, tired soul
Your boy knows he's yours
His loved one, his own

The Day We Were Born

The day we were born angels sang to our moms
The most beautiful song they would hear

All of their live long days
And all of our growing up years

The same melody plays soft notes
In our hearts and our souls

It's familiar somehow in our mind
We know not from where it springs

This heavenly sound
We think it's a place in life's time

If we would hum these lovely soft sounds
With our mothers around

They would laugh with delight in their joy
Love's music plays on for all of our days
If we're still we can hear it nearby

God's hands were on us as he handed us down
To our mom who loves us beyond all

She knows her child is the blessing
Sent straight from God's heart
Through her soul

There's no love like a mother's for her sweet baby child
Nor one ever like God's up above

They are two of a kind
If there is such a thing

As perfection, their perfect love

His Arms

Arms wrapped tightly around us
It still quite astounds us
To know that he loves us so much

There's nothing quite like it
Do we simply invite it
Warm, snuggly and, oh, just so right

Warm, soft and enfolding
It's us he is holding
Do we dare to ask him for more

He surely will give it
It's our life.....just live it
And give others this much and more

Heaven's Door

Wisping, whirling, soft white and swirling
Clouds at heaven's door

Watching, dreaming, plotting, scheming
How can we live each day more

Angels caressing us, times are pressing us
As we rush to get through each day

While watching, dreaming, plotting, scheming
Let's not forget to take time to pray

Our Lord is above us
Oh, how much he loves us
We must not forget him each day

Without pausing a moment so God can just hug us
We hurry and scurry, raise quite a flurry
Let's remember to take time to pray

Our Very Own Angels

Hair short and hair long
They all sing the same song
It's music our heart's ears can hear

They come in and come out
They're always about
Stay till our end, true and true

Some tall and some short
They're all holding court
For us now and forever we know

They're with us at birth
Full of joy and of mirth
For our life that awaits us, you know

Down our life's path they lead, follow and wait
Throughout good times and bad times, some late
Surround us, they do, when we don't want them to
Protect till we reach heaven's gate

Heroes

Heroes among us
Quietly go
About living their everyday lives

They did what they did a long time ago
To save our world's children from strife

Pain and suffering, agony and worse
Would be on our plates today

If the heroes among us had not done what they'd done
Long ago and far, far away

They paid a price that we cannot conceive
That anyone would have to pay

To keep freedom at home
They gave up precious lives, limbs
And sanity
All in war's day

They walk heaven's highways
And roads here on earth
Walking proud and unnoticed at times

To their neighbors next door
They're just that old man
Whose stories give his life rhythm and rhyme

How life has changed,
How we quickly forgot
As time aged our heroes, every one

Think of the great debt of gratitude
We owe these fine gents
Who kept our freedom intact
Under God's sun

My Father

With my Father in heaven
I feel like eleven
Or is it six, seven or nine

He gathers me up in one quick fell swoop
And says that things will be just so fine

I love him and trust him
Feel warm and quite blessed
He smiles as I chase every whim

I do know my boundaries
He thinks I'm a quandary
This little girl lost without him

Along my life's travels
I've known that he follows me
Throughout every hither and yon

I feel him beside me
He does not berate me
When sometimes I feel that he should

He sees all my good points
Puts up with my bad points
You see, his love is everything good

God's Kids

God's kids know him well
He thinks they're just swell
He sits at their feet filled with wonder

How could he have known
How precious they'd be
They live in his heart, just under

His heart feels their laughter
And also their joy
His heart swells with love and with pride

He's created them all
But still looks in awe
At perfection perfected inside

He marvels at their faith in his heart
They're all in his lap every day

They'll stay there forever
As long as they live
On this earth and in God's home in heaven

We're all God's kids
Didn't you know
We only grow up in earth's eyes

Our lives are young always
In the family of God and in his home
In his heavenly skies

Friends

God gives us friends
To be with us till the end
Of life's trials and yes, of temptations

They walk on our way
And never do say
Things that hurt or cause us pain

True friends stay with us
Through life's horrendous storms
And never measure the toll

True friends never waver
Never count the hours
Of time that they continually gave you

They share from their heart
Never stopping to thwart
Your spirit or efforts of soul

They know you'll be there
When it's their turn to bear
Pain and sorrow that lands on their chair

Love's road goes both ways
Depends on today
Who needs love more than the other

Friend's hearts seem to know
Which way they must go

They've made the choice
There's no other

Grandchildren

Grandchildren are wishes we made on a star
Long ago and far, far away
When we were just a mite of a soul
On our journey to our life this day

They come like soft wisps on the air
We cannot believe what they bring
To our lives and to those all around us

They can make hearts sing
That don't know a tune
Cause of brokenness without and within

Their smiles light up hearts
That are hard and quite cold
Whose heartstrings had dried up, they thought

Grandchildren are footprints on sands of our time
And touches down deep in our souls

They can mend broken hearts
When they are a part
Of our spirit that feels tired and old

There's nothing quite like
The soft angel's touch
That we feel when they climb in our lap
They nestle right down, they know where they're safe
They're warm comfort for us in their nap

Grandchildren build bridges o'er chasms of hurt
In families with rifts painful and distant
Their innocent souls know no boundaries at all
They love each person who's in their life constant

They're God's gift to mankind
That travels through time
It's his way of helping us cope
With travesties, hurt, anger and fear
To help our lives make sense and to rhyme

Our Children

Our children are ours for only a while
They grow up and soon go away
But do not weep long
They are truly God's song
In his best melody to be played

He walks with them you know
Wherever they go
He leaves them not for a minute

They are in his great care
In their everywhere
So worry not they're his children infinite

They'll climb every hill
They encounter and
Will take him with them for sure

If they fall he will crawl
To save one and all
If it takes that to reach them my dear

So rejoice everyday that your children at play
Will be lovingly watched over time
They are his too you know
In sun and in snow
They are cared for
His love for them is sublime

Our Best Friend

He's our best friend
With us till the end
Of the rainbow
Or end of our lives

He knows you and me
You might think, maybe,
He lives right inside of our heads
He does that in part,
And lives, also, inside our hearts

He stays by our side,
You can feel him right there
Don't worry, let go of despair

We're a part of him, too
That's right me and you
Our family's the same love we share

God our Father sent him
To watch over us
And catch us if we start to fall

Oh, we'll stumble and trip
But, he won't lose His grip
Of our hand or our heart if it be

He loves us so much
He's there when we fear
Things that go bump in the night
He'll watch over us no matter the place
He'll dismiss every bit of our fright

So walk now in peace
His hand is in yours
In darkness and light of each day

He asks only this
Love him back if you will
And please, remember to pray

Prayer

Prayer is a place you can go for relief
It is also a place for your heart
Prayer welcomes you home anytime anywhere
It's the best place in life you can start

It's safe and warm there
Nothing can harm
It's just you and your soul and your God

Prayer holds you so close
Won't let you go
Until you have rested your heart

Softness and calm reside in this place
Regardless your journey thus far
Prayer waits for us all
If we do or don't call
It's patient and part of us all

We can call upon God
To refresh our souls, forgive us and give us new strength
He will come where we are, find our soul's path
For us he will go any length

The Gentleness of God

The gentleness of God caresses my very soul
His tender touch softly brushes my weary heart
He holds me so closely
And won't let me go

I feel so safe and secure here
Inside my loving God's heart
There is comfort in knowing
That from my side
He will never ever depart

His angels have whispered in my sleeping ear
That I am in his great wondrous care
How can I not face the world with great joy
Knowing he's sitting right here

My heart sings with joy and with wonder
When I think of the meaning of this
Who would ever have thought
That he'd land in my life
And bring such heavenly bliss

He's there when the bright morning's light
Bids nighttime adieu and farewell
I awaken with glorious joy
To remember that I'm God's own delight

If you're really quiet and still
You may discover it's true
That our great God from Heaven above
Is also sitting right next to you

One That We Love

When one that we love
Has slipped from God's glove

We must pray
For their tender care

They are lost
So it seems

From God's gracious dreams
We must keep our hearts on their cause

Their path may be dark
But know that God walks

Right by their side
Every day

He'll not drop his watch
As they stumble and scratch

An existence
Their own painful course

His son will shine through
As it does for me and you

No matter the route
That they take

It's your loved one
He'll protect

Will never forsake
His child
As his precious heart aches

Our Gift

What is your gift
You may ask so disarmed
Is it quite evident
Where is your charm

Can you reach out your hand
To someone in need
That gift is so grand
In God's eyes above

We all have the gift
Of sharing his love

It may mean you must
Travel a path you'd not planned

Sharing God's love
May just strand
You in such a way
You know not how to turn

We plan out our lives in a way
Suiting us

When he has our ear
It may just bust
Your bubble of life you have
Lived within

We seem to forget that we are
One with him
His child on this earth
Walks on a certain path

Remember be aware
Of the dark one's wrath
That walks in God's shadow

And opens dark gates
That beckon us in
Early or late

On our way to God's Kingdom
In our lifetime's way

Don't wrestle with God
Take his hand on your way

His precious gifts are yours
Here to stay
So share them
With all you encounter each day

They too need his love
And for them you need pray
For protection and shielding
From all that can harm

The power is yours
To disarm
All the hurts
And transgressions that await
One and all
Theirs and ours

Reach out
Use your gift
And answer his call

GLIMPSES OF CHRIST

His Father on Earth

His father on earth
Was quite filled with mirth
To have the Christ child for his son

It was not always like that
The beginning was sad
When he thought
Of what Mary had done

It was hard to believe
That she truly conceived
through divine intervention, she claimed

He tossed and he turned
Till he really learned
That her words were the truth
As she said

The child would be his
Until his young end
His father would silently weep

To know that his child
Would suffer with pain
To bring salvation
For people to keep

He watched his son grow
And soon came to know
His family would share
The pain too

That his son would soon bear
As he became a man fair
His time would come soon
True and true

His son's love would abound
To each village and town
People could not believe
This was him

He would gently affirm
That his message was real
And true
As the sea's bright blue brim

As he watched his son's life
Soon fill with strife
He prayed the same prayer
Each day

Be with him, I pray,
Every step of the way
For he is my dear son, too

Throughout all his days
He would venture to say
That his love was as strong
As his Father's in heaven above

His Father, up there
And I, too, share
His sorrow and for sure his love

But, he's mine though today
And I will not give him up
Till I have to tomorrow

My Son

He is my son, dearest part of my heart
My touchstone, my dearest child
You cannot just rip him out of my arms
And throw him to the crowd wild

Do not take him away to stand trial with the swarm
Of rabble and beggars and thieves
He deserves honor, respect, worship and praise
Not to be forced to his knees

The world needs him now more than ever
And I need his love even more
He was sent through my heart
For all our new starts
By our Lord up above who adores

He told me to love and to keep him
From harm and I have done just that
Please do not shame him in public
I simply could not bear that

Please do not treat him with cruelty
He is not of this world, you know
You cannot just take him away from us all
He belongs to the world up above

His path is so cloudy
And dark up ahead
I must spare him whatever I can

But, you must not take him from my aching arms
Our Savior, the King of the land

He will carry our burdens
And all of our woes

It is painful to watch his load heavy
He bears all of our sins, outside and within
And never complains of the levy

Our Sin

Our sin is so heavy
Could he possibly levy a price
To redeem every one

He did it you see
He saved you and me
With his love just as bright as the sun

Our sin cannot stand the strength of the man
Who walked surely down life's mortal path
He bore up every one
He is surely God's Son
And took on all Satan's wrath

Sin does not stand one single chance
Its only dance sure will be brief

God's love does abound
It is always around
On this earth to be true and be sure
Our sins are washed now and forever we know
Our soul's hearts are certainly pure

Rejoice in this thought
That it's really naught
That you or I could ever have done
To redeem our own soul
To be completely whole
We owe that to God's only son

His Feet

His poor feet had holes from pain now inflicted
On his body, his heart and his soul
His heart was just broken
By words that were spoken
Hell's depths he would very soon know

For us he went through this
So our lives could flourish
The story is ours to retell
And retell to our family
Friend, and yes, foe
So along the right path we can go

His feet strong and worn weary
Caused his heart to beat freely
And also his tears to flow down
Just knowing his path gave him pause and great wrath
While greeting each newly sprung dawn

His mother's heart aching and all the while breaking
Remembering tiny feet kick in the air
She knew his sweet feet would soon lead down the street
To take him away in despair

His earth home he'd leave
As his last breath would heave
His mother would cleave to his feet

She kissed them and said,
"He will soon come again. He will rise from the dead as we speak."
She knew ere she talked
She knew where he walked
With his newly born feet all astride

He stood tall to them all
Every one of them saw
His new body with holes still intact
He smiled as he rose
'Twas the tips of his toes
The last sight they would ever recall

His Robe

His robe worn and thin
Clings so closely to him
As he drags himself
To his own cross

He stumbles and tears
His robe unaware
Of the voices that cry out to him

This is his call
To save one and all
While garbed in this tattered and torn
Robe that will fall from his limbs on his crawl
And be draped with a crown of sharp thorns

His robe will fall down as the thorny sharp crown
Pierces his brow that is creased
He cries out to his Lord
Spare not the sword for my journey will soon be complete

His robe fell to the ground
There was such a sound like no other had ever been heard
Then as fast as it came not a sound would remain
There was silence and dark all around

The cloth would be taken as his mother's heart breaking
Was heard by the Lord up above
Her son was now one with his Father and won
Our lives for us each and every one

The Battle

The battle for souls has raged on forever
Since time has really begun

The forces surround us
Unseen, but still raging
One dark, one bright as the sun

Trials, temptations are there every day
Each night as we lay down our head
One offers salvation, the other only heartbreak and dread

We've been given the choice
By our Father above
And then were sent on our way

We wrestle with choices
Our hearts are quite torn
As we try to get through every day

At times we do stumble
Become quite humble
The dark things sometimes look light

Satan tries to confuse us
He continues to use us
If we choose him he gains much might

But God's glories and angels are there all around us
To help us withstand the dark call

If we choose the light, the kingdom is ours
Salvation is God's battle call

We'll be happy we chose
Our Father, who rose, to heaven's great kingdom on high

We will smile all our days
Sing wonderful praise
As Satan retreats, by and by

His Breath

His breath gave us life
Carries us through every strife
We encounter each day on our way

He breathed it right in
To combat all sin
Within each of us every single day

He breathes in and breathes out
There is not one doubt
He does it for us every soul

He cleanses us now
Lives inside of our soul to help us
Learn how to be whole

He gives us his breath
To relieve us from stress
And troubles as they come our way

We need only breathe in
And we are saved from all sin
As we breathe with him
And walk on his way

His Hands

His hands worn and calloused
One day holds a chalice
Of life giving wine from his blood

His hands always tender as they always render
Life's blessings among all and one

The sick, how they came, the blind and the lame
To be near the one who would call

Never knowing for sure if his touch really cured
Their ailments and pains all around

He knew who they were like he knows us today
And what ills we are suffering from

A sad broken heart, a spirit now lost
An illness crushing body and soul

His love touches all who are so encumbered
He reaches for us every day

We need only reach back
And take hold of his hand
And he'll walk by our side on our way

He'll always stay with us no matter what happens
He wants us on him to rely

His Back

His back, strong and lean
Scorched by the sun
Carried the weight of the world

Around him life swirled
As people recoiled
And jeered him that day long ago

He carries us still
As we climb every hill
As fast or as slow as we go

We need not climb hard
He has us on board
Each journey, each step, every hill

We need only reach out
There is not one doubt
He will pull us along now and still

His love bears us up
As we drink and we sup
With our Lord, what a wonderful thrill!

His Heart

His heart while still beating
A path now entreating
Us all to follow his way

We shun and we turn
Even though we yearn
To follow his heartbeat one day

His tiny heart grew
As we all came to know
Into one that has room for us all

We each have a heart
That cannot wait to start
As we listen each day for his call

Why then turn away
When he calls us each day
To go our own way down our path

It's simple, you see
We still sit at his knee
With his heart having room for us all

His Blood

His blood, shed quite freely,
Is our only hope really
For a life that is free and untroubled

We stew and we churn about how we can turn
Bad things from going to worse
It's really quite simple
Our Lord's love is ample
There's plenty for one and for all

It's there for the taking
Our Lord's heart is aching
For his people to open their arms
To his love that is waiting
It is his creating that keeps us all safe and quite warm

Blood shed for one and for all
Simply extends us the call
We simply need answer the door

To a life safe, enriching
If your life is missing
Get up reach your hand and stand tall

Walk with the man whose heart lies in your hand
Open your heart here and now
You won't be disappointed

Your new life anointed
You'll be happy you answered his call

The Temptation

The dark prince had Christ for only an hour
The darkest one all his life

Pain, trauma and heartbreak were there all around him
Cloaked by goodwill and things nice

He offered Christ power and all worldly pleasures
Could be his this very day

If only he'd lay down his allegiance to God
The dark prince whispered so sweetly and fey

He tempted and baited our Lord with a vengeance
He was determined to win this great round

But Christ held steadfast and would not relinquish
His holy and heavenly crown

His life he'd lay down for all people on earth
And would not be tempted one bit

He told Satan "Be gone" and cast him that instant
Back to the deep burning pit

Because he held steadfast for you and for me
We stand here on this very day
With the strength to say "No, Satan, Get thee behind me,
And never return, not one day!"

We have Christ's strength and armor and all
The blessings he's granted to us
We need not fear darkness nor temptation
We stand with the King over All!

ENCOURAGEMENT AND CONSOLATION

His Ear

The ear of God hears it all
Each tiny tear that falls
On earth or on shoulders across time

He hears cries, even sighs
And sobbing and more
As his people continue to cry

He hears our joy too
And laughter as well
He hears it all and just smiles

The miles through our life
Sound like music to him
Some happy and somber melodies

He hears our beating heart
While with him or not
No matter where on this earth we wander

We can try to lose his ear
He will just reappear
No matter our trail put asunder

Shake him we cannot
He knows our every plot even fore
We know it for sure

He listens for fear
Slipping ever so near
And will wrap love all around all
Ends of our sphere

Each newborn's cry
And each last breath when they die
Are heard by his ear every minute

Not a sound gets away
Without his hearing it play
The world turns and he hears all that's in it

Loud sirens that warn of catastrophe around
The corner or round the world
Alert his strong ears that all people's fears
Need his hand on their life
And also in it

The joyous applause of great music abounds
Makes his heart and his ears swell with pride
He smiles down on us all
Because he's the one who placed
Music and all joyousness with us inside

So think not that he won't hear
Your softest prayer
Or your loud and desperate plea

He hears all as we call
Or when we fall
In despair
Right down to our knees

He will listen to beggars and bankers and thieves
He will hear every one's journey on earth
His ear has been close to our heart
From our very start
From the very first minute of birth

So, trust this great God
Who's in our shoes trod
And knows us inside and out
Know that he's waiting to listen
To your deepest dreams
And will hold you no matter your route

God's Love

God's love is real
You surely will feel
The stirrings down deep in your heart

His love never leaves
Stays while you grieve
He truly will never depart

Open your eyes
And you will realize
That his love is steadfast and true

He died long ago
So your life can flow
With abundance so joyful so true

He rose for you also
So you may join him some day
So follow him closely and you will be with him
In his heavenly home one day

His Love

His love is as sure as the oceans that swell
It keeps us intact
No matter how we react
To life's journeys that can take us through Hell

His hand is upon us
Through all of life's travels
There are many for one and for all

He is there all the time
Without rule or rhyme
It's true, simply answer his call

He sees us through trials
He sees us through joy
He's there every step of the way

He's inside us you see
Inside you and me
He rejoices in us every day

You will see him for sure
If you open your door
To his love and compassion and more

It's so easy for us
Simply just trust
His wisdom and love every day

His love sees us through
Every problem and stew
He's there every step of the way

As we wake up each morn
We are simply reborn
With our Father alongside us each day

Anger

Anger takes us all at once
Consumes us in all but a flash

If anger has its way with us
Sad journeys we'll find
On our path

What brings it our way
Disappointment this day
Or that one
We can't remember which

All we know is one moment we're happy
And the next thing we know there's a switch

In our attitude life's outlook indeed
Directions in life can change

We need head it off
If we possibly can
Or our life may just rearrange

Christ's anger was great
At blasphemous times
Everyone knew where he stood

His anger, quite vented
Worked not against him
It was anger whose presence
Was good

Our anger disjoints us
Entangles our path
Blinds us to good things in life

The 'dark one' smiles
In corners of our lives
Awaiting the downfall of good

Anger can come from dark places below
Or from injustice in light of day

If anger enmeshes your life
Stop and remember to pray

For God's tender mercies
Can heal us
In body, mind and in soul

He diffuses anger's hold on us all
Can help mend our hearts
Till they're whole

Forgiveness is ours to share with our friends
And foes all around us each day

We meet both on our meander
Through this gift called our lives
We must just remember to pray

Thirst

We thirst for cool water
Our soul thirsts for more

The only well that can satisfy
Is inside heaven's door

It's a well, oh, so deep
We can all fill up

Our soul can be quenched
We can fill our cup

The water down deep
Is there for all people

We simply need offer our vessels freely
They will fill right up to the brim

They never will empty
Thanks be to him

He waits by the well
That has waters alive

So drink up
Be sated

Our true life has arrived

Deep Hunger

We hunger for peace and calm
In our lives

Where can we rest for awhile
We live at warp speed

As we rush through life's door
Never thinking we may not come back by

We may not see the day after tomorrow
We hardly see this one today

Afraid we'll miss out
They whirl by in a blur

Do you remember two days ago now
I didn't think so, somehow

Sit still and be calm
Enjoy what you have
This day and this very night

We may not remember
This day's gifts from God
Who brings us joy and light

If continuing to rush through
Is the mode of our life

It just may pass us by like a thief in the night

Trouble

Trouble seems to find us
Wherever we are
We cannot avoid it
Even wishing on our star

It seeps under doorways
Climbs all mountains of stess
It knows exactly where we are
It's found our address

We can't run from trouble
We have tried and found
The very best thing
Is to face it right down

Look straight in its eye
Stand toe to toe
Ask your God who's always right by your side
To accompany you on this painful ride

He'll carry us over and under
Around and yes, even through
He won't let painful trouble
Ever get the best of you

If you ask him for help
And get down on your knees
Trouble will fly away with the breeze
That blows from God's wide open heart

His hand has your life's rudder
Just let him steer
Your troublesome course
It will just disappear
On its sleek black horse

It won't darken your doorway
For a day and awhile
It knows that you're God's heavenly child

When it does come again
You'll be ready, you see
You'll be stronger because down on your knees

You're arm in arm with your God
Each and every day
He will clear your troubles
Off and away

They'll leave for now
And when return you'll be stronger
Days will be bearable
Your endurance will be longer

You've the best partner of all
Right by your side
So invite God along on your life's ride

Our Tears

Our tears are for naught
Because he has bought
Our lives on a wing and a prayer

His sweet blood was shed
So we may be led
To lives that are truly a prayer

Dry your sad eyes
And you'll soon realize
Your sins are washed white as the snow

Life's journey is sweet
With a lovely retreat
To the end of the road you will go

His love will await
As you come toward the gate
To enter your heavenly home

Your family is there
On a wing and a prayer
To embrace you with their heavenly glow

The Storm

While raging around us
Life's storm tries to unground us
Disrupt all our peace and our calm

No need to worry
The storm's screaming fury
Can't touch us
We're in his great palm

The waves and the winds
That would blow hearts wide open
Can't harm us with his tender care

They scream all around us
While God's love surrounds us
We've nary concern or a care

The storm will blow over
And then come again
Hoping to catch us off guard

But it doesn't see that we always will be
Wrapped in God's great big wonderful arms

Life's full of storms
Big and some small
But we've nothing to fear at all

Storm warnings abound
God's always around
With him we stand strong
And stand tall

The Ocean

The ocean holds the power of God
With every wave that breaks

The swell of each one
Can make our hearts tremble and quiver and quake

Yet the gentle surf brings a calming surge
So soft you can feel your heart beat

But the power of the sea is something to behold
Never trust peaceful waters complete

For under the surface lie fathoms deep
Life streams we cannot comprehend

The depths of God's heart are just like the sea
Except his has no bottom or end

Currents can deceive
You may think you're close to shore
When you're leaving the safety of land

Alone in the sea can be a frightening place
But know that God is holding your hand

Look closely now
You may see his face
In each curl of the thundering waves
That toss you from shore to sea

Just ask for his help
For his lifeline to reach
And save you from the perilous deep

He's within your reach
Call out his name and
You'll soon be embraced on God's beach

His Eyes

His eyes are upon us
They constantly watch us
To make sure that we're safe and sound

They follow us always
Through dark and light hallways
While we just keep running around

He really does love us
From high up above us
We just need to take time to see
He holds our small hands as we travel the land
And holds us upon his great knee

His warmth wraps around us
As life keeps on making a fuss
We twist and we turn
While all the time yearn
For his face just to shine upon us

We don't even see
It is his face we feel in the wonderful warmth of the sun
We just need to look
It's our sins he took
As he trudged up the hill Calvary

His Kingdom

His Kingdom is ours at any time
His glories just outshine the sun

It's ours for the taking
It's all in God's making
It's something we've already begun

The heavens will open the door to God's Kingdom
If we will only reach right inside

We'll be with the Savior
From this day forever
Our love will be taken inside

In an instant our hearts will be soaring
In fact they will swell with such pride

To know that he takes us just as we are
It's the gift we never could buy

He loves us forever and will never sever
Our ties that make us so blessed

Our family is waiting for us at the door
They see us from quite afar

It looks far away as you search every day
You'll reach it by seeing your star

Your place is awaiting
Your dreams keep creating
Your most wonderful thoughts will appear

So when your time comes you'll know it for sure
You'll just go and thank God that you're there

Illness

When we are struck down
Malady in tow
Unaware that we would be stricken
Our mind tries to absorb the shock and the fear
That our body has already envisioned

Unable to believe that it's happened to us
We try to understand why
Since we've led such a clean and unfettered life
This has visited us at such a time

Acceptance comes slowly
Or not at all
Belief that it's here is still distant

We are face to face with our God
Is it time for us really to listen

We resist it at first
How dare this happen

We were just settling down in our life
Our plan did not include illness
This is definitely not part of our sight

When shock wears away
And reality sets in
We have come to a point to decide
How will we deal with this time in our life
How is it that we will ride

The storms and the trials that may come our way
One thing is for sure
This is the time to pray

God has told us that he will always be with us
We took him for granted when well
We could not have bargained that we would really need him
As we contemplate health's ride into Hell

Though we may not go there
We need to be armed
With God's tender mercies
And safe loving arms
That hold and keep us
No matter the outcome

If recovery is not sanctioned
He's with us through that

But it may be that our earth's time is not over
A blessing such as this
We truly hope we will find

Our fear of the unknown is paramount
The number one thing on our mind

We need not fear anything
For our God is with us
He will carry us throughout all our time

Crossing Rivers

Crossing rivers and fording streams
We all make our way somehow

Though rivers may rage
And streams overflow
Along life's way we go

If we've learned to swim
Through dark waters and deep

Our soul's load does not weigh us down
As much as if we'd not learned
Just how to carry life's load around

No matter what comes
Our way down our path

The Lord holds us up in the fray
Flooding banks through our life
Will not cause us strife
As we trudge through deep waters each day

You'd think as we grow
Life's ease would appear
Not so, we've found to our surprise

With God's hand upon us
With each growing year
We grow stronger, if not necessarily wise

If we listen to him and just take his hand
As we drift further and further from shore

Reaching new life in God's heavenly home
Will not be such a difficult chore

Warm waters and cool, whatever we need
Await us within Heaven's realm

We will lie down near the stream of love and goodwill
Glad that through life's waters we gave God the helm

Peace

God gives us peace
We only need ask

It's within our grasp every day
He asks one simple thing of us all
To live our lives his way

He's told us he's the way, the truth, and the life
We know that it's true if we try
To open our eyes to see God's love
And let him walk by our side

He does so you know
Whether we want or not
He does not leave us for a minute

We'd all be much happier on our walk through life
If we had our Lord deep down within it

So reach out your hand
And peace will be yours
Along with calm and rest

He gives us his all
At any time
This is surely his best

Spirit

Spirit moves us all of a sudden
When we least expect a jolt or a nudge

It's spirit that keeps us going along
Down our life's trail
Be it short or it long

Spirit moves softly, quietly through time
We can feel it at moments
Short moments in time

We must be really still to catch it at all
Spirit knocks often but whispers its call
For us to live lives that are spirit-filled

God's spirit lives in us
Oh, what a thrill!

Spirits

There are Spirits we love who watch over us all
And we know not when they are present

It's often I think
Sometimes I watch and then blink
Just trying to not be so hesitant

Their presence is near
We can capture it all and its essence

They're probably with us
Day in and day out
Hovering close to our soul

Our minds and our hearts
Have eyes of their own

Spirits come close
When we are all alone

These spirits are gifts that God's given
To savor and cherish

They're ours alone throughout all our lives
And live on even after we perish

Spirits help us live lives and yes learn
About love, commitment and such

Thanks be to God who lives up above
And blesses us with his spirit and touch

Food for Our Soul

Food we need for our soul
To make us all whole
Is abundant if we just open our eyes

It's ours for the taking
Our Lord's heart is breaking
To see us just pass it by

It's all around us
It absolutely surrounds us
We act like we don't even see

The life giving fruit
From his spirit and heart
That is waiting for you and for me

He is patient you see
With you and with me
As we go down life's path all alone

It need not be so
He's with us you know
He lives in our heart, his home

He waits for the day
To just hear us say
I hunger, I thirst for your Word

He smiles down on us all
As we answer his call
And opens his arms to our world

Our Fear

Our fear need not stay
God is with us each day
With him nothing can bring us great harm

If we ask our dear Lord
To stay in our world
And protect us and keep us warm

Fear cripples and harms
If we let it alarm
As we go through each of our days

We need tell it 'Be gone'
We are God's own
He protects and guards every one

Fear comes silently
It disarms us at times
We sometimes just cannot go on

But with God by our side
We can walk tall astride
And with no fear greet each day's new dawn

God's Link

God's link to your soul
Cannot come apart

Strong forces can never destroy
The tie that binds God's hand to your heart
His love will just never let you go

Heartbreak and trauma and pain may arrive
In doses you cannot believe

He'll still hold you close in his arms every day
It is you that he will never leave

Temptations will come
Temptations will go
Some will stay in your world

You need not fear falling
His hand will hold yours
No matter your path sad or no

Be it dark, be it light
Be it short be it long
God's love will now and forever keep you strong

His love is tied to our heart till our end
God our Father
Our soul mate our friend

Roads

Roads lie before us
Some look quite benign

Some look like perilous turf
We tend to not look at most roads we travel
We just go along as we wish

If we look very closely the roads tend to merge
They can look inviting at first

The roads that we travel when we do hunger
Look different than they do when we thirst

The roads in the desert have flowers that bloom
In the rocks and the dry arid grit

The roads in the forest look lush and green
Sometimes there's danger within it

Things are not always just what they seem
Roads can call with a real siren's song

Take care where you trod
Some roads lead to God

Some lead to a place that brings pain
It is sometimes hard to distinguish your course
When your life is continuous rain

If your life is in sun your choices can steer
You right off the road where you want
You may not even know when you veer

Take time, deeply breath
Look inside your heart
Do not be in such a hurry

If you ask God to guide you, he surely will
His love will come down in a flurry

As his child he will lead you down the right road
Not that you won't have a choice
But you won't go astray
No, not one day
If you listen only to God's voice

Sorrow

Sorrow laid in my lap
Like a big sleeping cat

It felt strangely comforting there
As I watched myself slip and slide
Into the land of despair

God lifted my weary heart and my soul
As I always knew that he would
All that I really needed to do was
Give him my soul for good

The choice was mine
I kept it for years
I held on tight throughout all my tears
That I shed over love's loss
And over grief that leveled my being

Mountains that needed to move
Helped me climb
Right out of my perilous groove

I realized that I would soon be asunder
If I did not reach right now to my God
Before I went all the way under

I raised up my hand to heaven above
And he picked me right up with his heavenly love

Living inside God's heart now
I wonder how long I'd have lasted
Without his lifesaving grasp

Definitely, I know not long
I was in very tough shape

Only one step
And I would have walked
Into the dark side of life's gate
And that I would have lived to regret

Flowers

Flowers bring comfort
When souls are sighing
And crying and trying to heal

Tiny little blossoms poking up through snow
Bring hope for God's children who live here below
The heavens above where God's heavenly love
Reaches down for us all
And we land in his soft glove

On warm summer days
Bright blossoms sing
To our heart's delight
Somehow we know
No matter what comes
That we will be all right

God's messages come through soft petals and leaves
They've fallen from his garment
From his heavenly sleeve

They land on our sorrows
Disappointments and more
They bring riches to beggars
Lift spirits quite poor

They thrive among rocks and dry riverbeds
Don't be deceived
When they bow down their heads
They're probably resting or worshiping their maker

We need take a lesson
They can be our life shaker
We rest not enough
Don't worship our God
Nearly enough as we know that we should

In our shoes he's trod
He knows of our anger
Depressions and pain
That's why he sends beautiful flowers from rain

Flowers are soft messages sent from above
That we're never far from his wrap around love
He holds us, enfolds us and scolds us
Though gently
We are safe in his bouquet
So incidentally

Spend time in a garden
Yours or some other
You'll sense your God's love

He loves all earth's brothers
And sisters as well
All over his map

Relax, rest your heart
You're one of God's flowers
Blooming safely in his lap

Bridges

We need build bridges where love takes us not
Wide chasms unspanned
Lie deep down in our heart

If we reach cross the caverns of time and of hurt
Glorious joy may await us
If we'd just span the girth

Spanning distance seems not possible at times
Our heart feels

But if we reach not out daily
We may just not feel
The happiness and goodness
That life may reveal

God knows that that journey
Is necessary
And more

Bridges cross many a mile
That may lie uncharted

For completeness of life
We must now get started

Reach outstretched arms
To bridge hurts time has wrought
Just think of Christ's bridge
And just what he bought

For us one and us all
From the hill far away

Without his bridge-building
Where would we be today

His bridge reached o'er Hell's gates
Onto heaven's bright shore
He carries us across

He even bore
Our pain and life's sorrow
By spanning that breach
We must now cross our own bridge
That we inevitably reach

On life's journey that takes us
Far and away
We'll look back now and then
And undoubtedly say

The bridges I burned lie in ashes all 'round
What I wouldn't give for one soft little sound

Of the love and devotion
I may have received
Had I not burned the bridge
That was right on my sleeve

I thought I knew best
The path for my life
Had I crossed Jesus' bridge
I may have just sliced

The fear and the sorrow that came to my door
But hindsight's behind me
I must journey on more

And cross all the bridges
That will soon come my way
With God's hand in mine
I will meet them with courage
Each single day

Places in Time

There are places in time
Where I go in my mind
When my thoughts are quiet and soft

They are far and away
In a long ago day
When life was so simple
With thought

I travel back
When my current life lacks
The soft and warm places like there

It comes when I rest
Or when I'm at my best
Quietly relaxing in my chair

There are people there too
Who I once really knew
Cared about me and held me so close

They've gone on now I know
To heaven's bright shore
I will see them when I also go

Will they remember me too
I hope so and true
Are my memories
I hope I'm in theirs

God gave me places in time
Happy and sublime
To hold on to through life's heavy climb

He gives us what we need
Knows exactly what that is
Before we have given it a thought

Pray to him up above
Give him thanks for his love
And for the wonderful place in his heart

Bridging the Gap

How does love bridge
Years of pain
And of loss
One feels in their heart this day

It seems we would love
Those placed in our lives
By our Father in heaven above

It's not easy you see
I say down on my knees
To open my wounded heart

Years of envy and lacking
And being second place
Have driven life's wedge
Through my heart

Blood's thicker than all
I've heard it said
But bad blood has tainted my soul

I feel so empty and so left out
How can I again feel whole

I've put distance and miles between family
And distance twixt heart and of soul

I must get back to love's place in my heart
Because there is such a large hole
Where softness and warmth once settled in
I remember from long, long ago

How far did it run
Or was it me that had begun
Building walls to block out love's sun

My family is there
They are quite aware of my sadness and anger and sorrow
If I walk in love's door right now and right here
Would they love and welcome me even tomorrow

I must take the chance
I know that life's dance
Can be short and bittersweet if we tarry

I best pack my heart and head to heart's home
I believe there's love abundant for sharing

Should I do it right now
Or should I think more somehow
And maybe they'll make the first move

The first step's the hardest
I'll hold my God's hand
His voice while soft is the loudest

He'll stand
By my side as I walk through that door
Of forgiveness, understanding and love
In moments I'll feel like I never left

I remember my hand in mom's glove
She held me so tight
Never let me go
How could I remember that not

God's hand holds me still
I wonder if she will
Remember when we were in that spot

I will take the chance
And dance the next dance
Into family's welcoming arms

While God holds us all
We will stand close and tall
And embrace love's return
One and all

Sidewalks

Cracks in sidewalks are like cracks in our life
It takes a strong blow to break concrete
And bring rife to the fissures of our life

Is it the long wear and tear of time
That splits our foundations
That splinters life's rhyme

Winter brings frost and heaving and more
Springtime brings thawing
And that does implore
Us to wish for summertime's hot warming sun

Changing temps take their toll
Constant change wears
On tight seams
That keep our life whole

Our bodies like sidewalks can only
Stand so much stress
One final blow
Can brings us duress

If we're not careful to pick up the pieces
We may lose precious memories
And long ago faces
From times in our lives that were simpler somehow

Can we find them again before
Life's curtain bow

Cracks can be sealed with glue and with mortar
Our soul's seams are tender
And we ought to garner
God's healing touch right here in our grasp

We need only reach out
And simply ask
Our Father above to caress us with love
He'll do so in a minute
He lives in our lives and
Leaves not for a minute

So follow your heart and follow your soul
Hand in hand with your God
Your walk will stroll

On smooth walks through life
Down many a path
Sweet comfort is yours
Rest now and relax

Going Home

Going home is what we'll do
When our time on earth is through

Not alone we'll find on our way
God holds our hand
We know this very day

Fear and sorrow we'll leave behind
Memories of love are what we'll find

As we pass from life's door
Through the other

We'll see our father and our mother
Brothers, sisters, friends all abound

With their soft love
Arms wrap around

To welcome us
To our rightful place
God holds us close
And shows his face

He's smiling now
And tears of joy
Will softly fall
Upon your brow

As he holds you near
His heart and soul

You'll smile now
Your life's journey is whole

Signs

A soft touch on your shoulder
A gentle nudge in the night
God's whispering to your soul

He sends down His angels
To watch over us
To help with our illusion of control

Wherever we turn
The hard ways we learn
Could all go away in a flash

Some pain we may avoid
If our heart's ears were wide open
And one single word we'd catch

Firm pushes may come
If our hearts don't hear
The soft angel's brush of her wing

Silent or still
Chances are that we will
Hear those who watch o'er us and sing

But rarely we listen to our angel's lips
That hover so close to our soul

We oft turn away
And walk our own way through our life
With its pain and its woe

Signs come and signs go
We may never know
The joys we have lost
Living inside our bubble

If we'd just walk with God
His blessed path we'd trod
And avoid much pain and much trouble

Signs come every day in many a way
They're around every bend in the road

They are there to help us
Avoid troubled waters

If we listen
We may be spared heavy loads

God sends them through angels
In whose care we reside

They try to take us closely aside
From the danger that lurks all around

Or the problem that looms
Now and then

We just go on our way
Each and every day
Not seeing the pits we fall in

Some signs are sent
To show us the light
That will bring us great joy in our life

If we choose to ignore
We may pass through the door
Of sadness and peril alive

So open your ears
And just try to hear
The messages sent from above

God sends us great things
Gives us our wings
To fly off to our life and his love

Restless

Sleep will not hold me
My mind will not rest

I know not what's binding
My soul's needed rest

It is now nighttime
When I normally lie down

But my soul will not let me
Find peace and calm

Is God trying to reach me
His message to tell

I'll sit here so softly
Perhaps I'll hear God's knell

My heart's been so tired
Body, soul too

Why don't I simply listen to you
Trying to tell me to slow down my pace

I seem to get caught up in life's wild race
For what purpose I think to myself with a query

No wonder every inch of me
Feels, oh, so weary

Slow down every step
That you take from your place

We'll find much more pleasure
Maybe we'll see our life's face

Will it will smile through our days
And softly hold nights

I think rest will find us
Give us pause from the strife

Of hustle and bustle
Competing with time

Slow down, breathe in life
Try to savor each sublime

Minute that comes with your way
On your path

We know not when
Life's minutes may too soon dash

Away from us all
It may be gone in a flash

Listen to God's soft voice
In the night
He'll sooth our hearts

Give us rest from the flight
That we feel everyday...
Pray for peace in your nights

Death

When death gently knocks
On the door at your place

Have no fear now
You will soon see God's face

Softly wrapped in his arms
All peril and pain
Will leave in a flash
Your joy will now gain

You may now lay down
Your tired weary head
On God's welcoming lap without dread

When life plays its final song
It sounds like music so sweet

Tears of joy fill your heart
And will gently fall on your soul

Your eyes now see so clear
Your path from this place

Your place on this earth
Will be filled
With loving warmth straight
From the heart of God's grace

And memories of all you hold dear
Loved ones you leave
Will join you one day
On their journey to heaven from here

Your reason for living your time
On this earth
You simply will now understand

Your life will have purpose and rhyme
Questions you've had
Swirling around in your head
Will now have answers you'll find

So lay down your head
Close your eyes
Take his hand
It's time to come live
In God's holy land

Anguish

There's a place between anger, grief and despair
Life takes us there
Before we're aware

Our travels through life
Are uncertain at best

When anguish comes calling
We can only behest
Our thoughts and our fears
All mounted on top

One on the other
When will they stop
Attacking my heart and my soul and my being

I look to my God
O please hear my plea

I have pain all around me
I know not which way to turn

Life's lessons escape me
Guess I didn't learn

The lessons out there
Awaiting us all

If I had learned
I doubt that my fall
Would be so hard or so far

From what I feel is God's grace
Is it possible he will still show me his face

Even though I am lost
Like the lambs long ago

I'm out in the bramble
Caught from below

Will he hear my cry
And save me from this

I need rescuing soon
I can't live like this

Betwixt hell and heaven
I feel I must go up

I should have listened
Not drank from the cup

Of sorrow and heartbreak
That I did so many a time

If I can just have a chance
I promise I'll climb
Right out of this pit
That I have fallen in

Please reach right down
And save me from my sin

My anguish lets up not
I never knew such a place
Could ever exist
Turned away from God's face

I feel his forgiveness and life saving love
Breathing into my soul
Filling my empty cup

Thank God, you heard me
From way up on high

Your lamb is safe now
Look at how blue the sky
Appears at my glance
On my knees I'm so thankful
I've joined God's sweet graceful dance

Empty Heart

Is your heart feeling empty
Is it tough to go on

You're not alone
Many people seem gone

Gone from God's ways
And his truth and his life

People seem muddled
And all caught up in strife

God's waiting right here
With his arms open wide

To hold and enfold us
Each day inside

We need only reach back
With our outstretched arms

Take Christ as our Savior
Let him walk in our life

It's really quite simple
We make it so hard

Just reach out your hand
Right to your Lord

Who loves you from birth
Spans all the girth
Of trials and of temptations

He'll carry you through
What you must muddle through
To get rid of your lamentations

Rest with ease
Fill your heart

It will be empty no more

He'll fill it right up
Overflow your cup
With forgiveness and lovely sensations

94

LIFE TODAY

Rocks

Rocks in our shoe
Rocks in our path
Things that rock our soul

Boulders that block every way that we turn
Can frustrate and make us anger prone

Building with rocks can shore up our walls
Provide us with shelter we need

Where are the stepping stones that we want
To help find our way through the weeds

The rolling stone that gathers no moss
Can get in our way at times

A stone that won't stay put in its place
Can unsettle our rhythm and rhyme

Peace cannot be found
If we leave no stone unturned
We will be looking for 'we know not what'

Sometimes it's best to stack rocks in a pile
And leave a rockslide lay where it should

The rock that was rolled in front of Christ's tomb
Was meant to stay there till the end

No rock could confine him or his love to be shared
Soon all knew he was not at his end

Stones that are thrown to hurt and to maim
Need quickly be laid to rest

How can we hurt with words that are spoken
And weave through life God's thread

We need take a page from God's Book
Find stones that we've thrown and make peace

Mend fences that anger's torn down
Give your tired soul some release

Stones can build walls where none need to be
Walls can divide and raise havoc

The world needs God's peace
Not chaos and people quite manic

Stone altars will fall if we've built them for worship
Of something other than God

He, alone, is our Savior
Our one rock that matters
Cling to him and his behavior

Waters

Waters can wash us with bubbles galore
They can wash us away in a storm

Still waters may consume when we look not
Wild ones may take us down not

Warm waters can soothe us when we need the rest
Cool waters can relieve pain

Waters that cleanse can bring us much joy
We can find delight in the rain

Pleasure may come from a day on the sea
Just when we need such a pause

Our world may be a thundering roar
Inside the waterfall
Where we are definitely lost

Oh, we can tread in waters deep
Shallows may take us to our end
We just never know where we can float
Water can be our best friend

We need it for life
We need it for faith

We baptize with it every day
On it or in it or sprinkled by it
May show the role God asks us to play

We can soak in streams, brooks and deep rivers
Much to our heart's content

It's when we get in waters quite over our heads
That we soon may have things to regret

If we learn to swim when it is safe
And tread water when it is not

God will swim with us all the way through our lives
And will carry us when we cannot

Young People

Young people struggle with life every day
Tough decisions come & go their way

Uncertainty, mistrust, faith and despair
Await each young person as they open their door
To their life each day as it appears

It pains them and breaks them at the same time
Why doesn't their life just easily rhyme

Friends come and go
Through life's swinging door
Where is the happiness
They thought was in store

For their lives that were given them as a gift
If that is so
Why doesn't it lift
Their hearts and their souls that need it so much

Just where is this God who appears at a touch
They need him this day, can't wait a minute
Their lives feel so empty if he's not in it

Temptations abound at each corner's turn
Peer pressure excruciates
They toss and they churn

Sleep is elusive
They don't know the way
They should go right now
Much less the next day

Their parents don't hear them or see them pass
Their own lives come first
Kids are second or last

Depends on the day
Or the wind's blowing way
Their tasks at hand
Or the lay of their land

Tomorrow they'll spend time
With their children, they say
But tomorrow may come and the young go away

They're off to live lives of their very own
Seldom they call or visit their home

What was there to keep their home in their hearts
Their families were distant or simply apart

They may have shared the same space on the block
But their drummers were different
They watched different clocks

Parents were off and away on their travels
Their kids left behind with lives to unravel

Is it too late
To bind back the bond
Of parent and child
Will the children respond

It's never too late to try
Yet to reach them

Get down on your knees and ask God
And beseech him
To reach cross the rift of time and of miles

You know, we are also his heavenly child
We may have wandered afar and away
Not unlike our kids that our hearts yearn for today

He will not forsake us
Do not forsake yours
We must keep open our heart and home's doors

Winds

Winds come and go
Some bring change and bring calm
Some winds can be terror-filled

Warm winds bring peace
Cold winds can bring fear
But God's winds will bring us to him

Hear the wind howl, cry and its screech
Hear it sooth babies to sleep
God's winds will lull us and keep us at peace
If we trust him when we at last sleep

So, rest, close your eyes
Have not a care
The night will be peaceful and calm
God's hand's on you now
He's caressing your brow
He will bring only sweet and soft balm

Windows

Windows help us look out or look in
Depends on where you are today

They say windows are the eyes of the soul
Which one will you open today

We know that when one window shuts with a bang
Another one opens somewhere

We have to look hard to find it sometimes
Often it takes a little prayer

One usually opens where we would not look
It's truly a mystery

You'd think that it would be easy to find
But not necessarily

Let your heart open like curtains that billow
When warm summer winds saunter through

You won't be dismayed
At the wonderful things
That will undoubtedly happen to you

Windows come in rounds and in squares
Some octagon and other shapes

The different angles of life's journeys
Will appear as through them you traipse

Don't be thrown by the odd ones
They may be plenty
The straight and narrow are there too

It depends on God's wonderful plan
That he has in store for you

You have his heart and have his soul
You have his promises too

Trust him, take his hand and he will guide you
All the wondrous way through

Our Earth

Our earth screams with pain
As man counts his gain
From polluting our air and terrain

God sees from above
And cries, all in love,
What does man hope to possibly gain

Man is selling God's soul
By destroying the whole
Health of the world that God made

The earth's creatures are dying
All of earth will be crying
Once man sees what greed has ordained

It will sadden us all to watch our earth fall
Into ruin, as it surely will
We can stop it you know

God sees man below
And prays that his love will awaken
In time before the earth's breaking
Our world as we have come to know

God yearns to impart
His love to man's heart
To stop all the pain he now sees

It makes God's heart sad
Watching greed make man glad
As he forgets to get down on his knees

We all have a part in listening to God's heart
Let us stop and see damage thus far
We can turn it around if we all gather round

God's heart is waiting for you and for me
We must join our hands
To restore the land
And the waters in peril right now
Turn your heads to the sky
And ask yourselves why

The answer will soon be made known
We're earth's children and God's
And all part of his plan
We are his, yes, his very own

Family

Show love to your family
With every beat of your heart
Too soon they are gone from our midst

Loved ones we take for granted
Thinking they will be always be here

Cherish each moment you have them
Tell them you love them and care

None of us knows when heaven may call
To say that we're needed there

Mend any fences you need to
Solve problems as soon as they come

Each day is so precious
With your family on earth
Savor them every one

They are in our lives for a reason
We may never know what it is

God gave them to us to have and to love
He knew we would need them someday
To help us get through this thing called life
And ease pain that may come our way

Heartstrings are far reaching
And strong as steel
They can reach through time if needed

Love them now
Love them ever
Tell them often and more
What they mean to your life
How you care

This love will come back to you three hundredfold
Love will stay when they are no longer there
God gave them to us
As his precious gift
He wanted his best to share

Life's Wind

Life's wind is so cold
It chills to the bone
Why won't it just leave me
Just leave me alone

It blows all around me
No matter the way
I walk down life's path
Not even if I stray

Away from the howling
Blustering blow
I wrap my cloak
Around me to shield me somehow

It's God's cloak I need
To wrap round myself
Why couldn't I see this
Myself on the shelf

Of time and of travels
I sat there for years
Stuck by my traumas
And all of my fears

I ventured down from the precipice
That held my life close
I thought if I stayed there
That I was safe from life's ghosts

The ghosts of lives past
And of future
They loom
Around my heart's pain
There just wasn't room

To let in the light
That shines from up above
I closed my weary eyes
And hid from God's love

He found me
And picked me up in his arms
And told me he loved me
And that not one bit of harm

Would touch my life now
That I was his own
I'm wearing his armor
And his glorious crown

That started with thorns
A long time ago
I heard that story once
But I'd let it all go

Alongside life's road
As I traveled along
Missing God's love
And his lifesaving song

But I have it now
Right inside my heart
I know that from me
He will never depart

So let life's winds blow
They can't touch my life
I am shielded from all
With God by my side

My Demons

I wrestle with demons
From without and within
No matter my travels
They seem to seep in

To my weary heart
And soul that is waiting
To rid itself of this evil
This evil contemplating

Its next move
To hinder my life in some way
I try to elude it
It just won't stay away

I try to hide
Inside of my heart
It finds me right there
I want it to depart

Oh God I implore thee
Take this trial from me
I ask from my heart
On my bruised bended knee

Take this trauma
And cast it away from my life
I ask for my family
Protect us from strife

It's your tender care
That we need in our home
Not sadness and heartbreak
That somehow just roams

From chamber to chamber
Within our life
Please walk with us on our journey
And protect our precious lives

The Lost and the Lonely

The lost and the lonely will stay that way only
If we don't stop to reach out our hand

His hands pulled us up when we were so down
That the bottom was where we looked from

Remember, his child, that his love, while so mild
Expects us to follow his lead

There are people who need us
As we always need him
So reach out and extend your hand

When you lift someone else it comes back in ways
You will cherish for all of your life

So, reach to a soul that is needy of heart
And whose life has such pain and such strife

It takes such a little part of your heart
To share what he has given you

So, find someone who needs you and pass it on through
And his heart will be smiling too

He has told us the poor will always be with us
Poor in spirit as well as life's place

That's where his heart lives
It's truly where he gives
His blessings and shows us his face

Fatigue

Exhaustion of soul
Being tired of mind
Our lives are wearing away

It takes such a toll
Of our hearts and our souls
To trudge through each and every day

We rest not enough
Don't lay down our heads
Through our nights and also our days

One day we'll wake up
With souls terribly frayed
And wonder why life feels this way

We rush and we push
To include everything
That we possibly can
Into lifestyles that can hold no more

God watches and says,
'My poor children down there,
Why do they live all these miles?'

His head must be shaking
And his heart must be breaking
To see us live life such a pace

If we'd stop just one minute
To see just what's in it
We'd probably glance at God's face

If we did so we'd see
That he's right at our knee
Just smiling and loving us so

Take 'five' now today
During work or at play
Breathe him in
And let God in your day

Life

Life comes to us as quite a surprise
We really don't know where we are

Until someone shows us the way to go
Take a deep breath and wish on a star

We march to the hustle and bustle out there
And wonder how we've come this far

Life takes us away with the winds of change
Which happens almost every day

In order to keep our feet on the ground
It's a real good idea to pray

Pray for your path and all of your friends
As they travel life's perilous course

None of us knows what awaits us out there
Some of us ride a dark horse

We fly through life's time in the blink of an eye
Before we know it we have grown old

So, now where is that rainbow and that pot of gold
It's a myth we discover much to our dismay

Life does not get easier now
The longer the climb, the harder it gets
To get through every day

The answer we had the day we were born
God's angels gave it to us

He's been with us every step of the way
It's in him we need put our trust

He's pushed us up hills and carried through valleys
We have been quite unaware

Of the partner we've had every day of our life
Who comes on a wing and a prayer

Lone Soul

Souls wander around
Up one street and down

Looking for peace
In our world

There is only one way
We find this day

To have peace
And keep it around

Us everyday
Wherever we stray

In darkness
In light of great day

God's hand is around
His love just surrounds

Us as our lives continue to fray
As we walk our lone path

We encounter wrath
Of one who would seek our downfall

And leave us to mourn
Our soul's loss reborn

Then God reaches to us
Lifts us tall

We then walk with him
Through thick and through thin

The evil can't touch us at all
Hold on to your Lord

It's through his powerful sword
Of love and forgiveness
We soar

In Between

In between heartache and trauma and more
Try to find happiness
That lies right in store

It awaits us with patience
It awaits us with solace
It knows our hearts are breaking
And knows our true trauma

The cracks are just splinters
Of time and God's love
It's there we can peek through
Feel his constant hug

That holds us and molds us
Right inside his heart
It's there that we learn
That he'll never depart

He's right by our side
Each hard step of the way
When we cannot see
He gets us through day

And gets us through nights
Where we truly are lost
He's right by our side
No matter the cost

He paid our price long, long ago
His climb was much harder
Than the way we now go

So, walk hand in hand
With the one who's right here
He hangs on so tight
He's always there

Poetry is Dancing

If poetry is dancing
My soul leaps with joy

If life is romancing
We all can enjoy

Yes, enjoy all God brings us
Upon each new day's dawn

Our hearts are a spinning
With love and much more

Much more we can give
To all lives whose souls touch

Our heart's full abundance
We have oh so much

So much we can share
With those whose paths we cross

We cross many paths
Whose hearts are in blush

Perhaps blush of pain
Or blush of great sorrow

We need do it today
And not put off till tomorrow

God touches our soul
And does cross our path

He caresses our blush
Doesn't wait til tomorrow

CLOSE TO HEART

My Little Girls

How I'd love to hold my little girls in my lap
Snuggled down all soft and so warm

Smelling like fresh fallen rain
It's my heaven below

When did they grow into women mature
People I'm proud to know

When did they walk women's way
Like I did
Was it when I turned my head

I used to lead them down life's path
Holding hands
One day they will lead me instead

They're my best friends on this very earth
And will live in my heart
Once I head for heaven's turf

Not too soon tho'
I'm not in a hurry

I want to just marvel
At my girls' lives
Who seem to be all in a flurry

They have little girls that they held in their lap
Young women and one single son

They too have my heart
And will never depart
No matter where their lives run

Mom's kids stay with us
It's them that we trust
To see us through this life's travails

We take turns with each other
Love's way knows no other
Way to give life to one another

Grief

Grief comes upon me when I least expect
It may be a call from a friend now and then

My mother's friend's voice will set me to tears
It brings back the memories of now lost years

And tears start to flow without any warning
I tend to forget that I'm still in mourning

No black armband I wear to alert those around
I just walk very lightly on grief's sad, sad ground

Sometimes I forget my loss in my heart
It's just now and then the sorrow again starts

Life goes along just so fine
For many a day

It's when I start thinking after I pray
For comfort and guidance
And strength from above
To live life without my loved one's love

Had I known how I'd feel along life's path
Would I have held my tongue longer
And not vented my wrath

At my life's disappointments
I blamed on my folks

Sometimes life looked like a terrible joke
Why did I have to live through
What I did
When I was a youngster
While I was a kid

How unfair, I thought that
My life did not go
The way that I wanted
Too fast and yet slow

I looked to others to blame
And to curse
I looked not at me
To see the reverse

Could I have altered my path
On my way
Perhaps I must deal with this this very day

God gives us our parents to launch us on earth
They're there to love and to guide us
On our way from our birth

When it doesn't go the way we think it should
Does it necessarily mean our life wasn't good
It's all in our perspective
The way we skew our view

If this hits you too hard
It might be that you
Need look deep inside
With realistic eyes

Search your life's path
And you may realize
That your life may have wandered
Down a different road

Had you heeded the call
And done what you were told
Follow your heart
And your soul will too trail

The responsibility's ours as well as
Those who we blamed for our fail
Of life and of love
We needed each minute

Life's joys and heartbreak
Are just in life infinite

Forgive those you blame
Let them rest in peace
Forgive yourself too and feel God's release

Heart's Pain

How can you describe
Someone's pain and one's loss
When a loved one is gone from their arms

The crevasse is deep
When pain there makes its home
Daylight does not in there seep

A piercing fine pain
Sears one's poor heart
Some days don't know
Just where they should start

To take one step
And then take another
One foot tries to move
The other stays still

Can't do it
And cannot recover

Knowing not when pain lands
Hearts wait on a shelf
Beating softly and fragile at best

No one told us ahead
This life's journey we'd tread

We could have prepared
Perhaps even spared
Heart's shock and life's brutal test

We must now go on
We meet each gray dawn
With sorrow and loss and tears all

Will it stop hurting one day
Will we once again say
Life will begin
We'll walk and will not fall

To our knees
And plead please

I am down on my knees
Night and day
Just trying to learn

How do I know
And how do I discern
The good from the bad
And also the pain from the loss

I put faith in above
And count on God's love
To get me through this and through that

He won't let me down
He's always around
Just be still and you're in God's lap

Mothers and Daughters

A paradox for sure
This pair of women
Joined together by birth

Look in the mirror
You each will see your surprise
How do you measure your worth

Once in time you sat on her lap
When did you change places with her

Once a little girl needing her mom
She now needs her mom even more
How does she make her way through this world
With her mom gone away from her role

The child is the mom now to her own mom
No one prepared her for this

The loss is tremendous
The pressure is worse
Coping is difficult at best

How unfair how unjust
She thinks in her anger
I have my own life to live

Then she remembers her mom being there
When she was just little and lost
Totally dependent on this woman for her life
It seems like just yesterday tossed

Did her mother feel anger in giving up so much
So her daughter could have life come her way
Maybe it's my time to take care of her
Like she took care of me every day

How soon we forget how love makes its way
When we each find ourselves in need

Home in my Heart

The mountains that beckon me home in my heart
Have stayed ever constant no matter my start

Away from this place on journey of heart
How could I have known from whence my heart's start

That took me away on journeys afar
In body and soul

Now I've come full circle
I feel close to whole

Wholeness of being is a path we unravel
As our steps go forward
And two steps back

Our lives feel full
And then empty

What do we lack
Adventures of old or break of the heart

We could not have known at life's first depart
From norm or lifestyle
We ambled straight and away
Turning this way and that on long ago day

Peace and warm places live deep in my heart
I know now from them I will never depart

SEASONS

Winter's Whisper

Winter whispers its secret
To my very soul

Its cold frigid message
Releases its hold

Once we both turn the corner
Of weary worn days

We can see spring upon us
We can now count the days

Our memories of frost
And wind's keening wail

Will be but a trickle
Spring lives will unveil

Our hopes grow for our lives
And our brother's as well

We begin to come out
From winter's hardened shell

We do seem to burrow
'Neath mountains of snow

No one can blame us
On this frozen turf below

Below our God's heaven
Up high in the clouds

Where winter not touches
It's nowhere around

Only springtime and summer
Live in God's holy land

We will see it with glory
Once we take his great hand

The Season

The season's upon us
It feels so very heavy
What joy can we feel
In our hearts

People in such a hurry
In a blur, in a scurry
Not a one is set apart

We seem to have lost
The reason we sing
The reason we praise up above

Between the ribbons
And crush of bright paper
We need to remember his love

His love came to us through
A tiny baby far and away
One whose path would be wearing and tough

Who brings salvation
This very day
To one and to all
No matter our steps how rough

No matter how far
We fall
From his grace on high

At the end of life's time
We'll soar through God's sky
To join all who have
Gathered above

The music they live
And yes also sing
Is of God's heavenly love

To each precious child
Who walks this sad earth
Who have been
In his tender care
Since their very own birth

When holidays come
With the pressures they bring
Just remember
God's wonderful love
And the release that he brings

The Lonely Couple

They feared for their lives
As they fled from their home
The place where their hearts Found God's peace

They ran for their lives
For their child unaware
God kept them
And brought them release

From harm's horrible way
They fled night and day
They were simply
Doing God's Will

Why is it that good
Is such a threat
Why do forces
Surround just to kill

To kill God's love
In places of good
Where sad hearts
Need it so bad

As they fled in the dark
Their donkey's head down
He plodded towards safety
And they prayed

Prayers whispered that night
On their fearful flight
Were heard
By their God on high

Angels held them so close
They felt their wings soft
Surround them
Each step of their path

No harm could come near
They now felt no fear
Evil can't stop
Cannot vent its wrath

The Child will be born
One day draped in thorns
But for now
He will only joy know

He comes from on high
He brings love and sighs
That one day
We will understand

Little family just born
Will always adorn
The world with God's grace
For our land

Give great thanks up above
For God sending His love
In the gift of a small little boy

This gift of a child
Will bring all of us home
With sweet rapture
And indescribable joy

"God's Ribbons" is Cynthia Watts' first book. Inspired by an enlightening experience surrounding her mother's illness and death she is pleased to share it with others. Cynthia is married, has two grown daughters and four grandchildren. She and her husband live in a small Midwestern community in South Dakota.